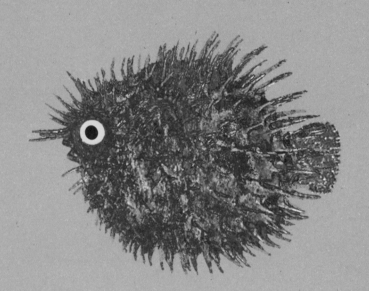

First U.S. edition 2019
First published by Templar Publishing (U.K.) 2018

Library of Congress Catalog Card Number 2018962219
ISBN 978-1-5362-0625-8

19 20 21 22 23 24 LEO 10 9 8 7 6 5 4 3 2 1

Printed in Heshan, Guangdong, China

This book was typeset in Core Circus
Rough and Neutraface Text.
The illustrations were created digitally.

BIG PICTURE PRESS
an imprint of
Candlewick Press
99 Dover Street
Somerville, Massachusetts 02144

www.candlewick.com

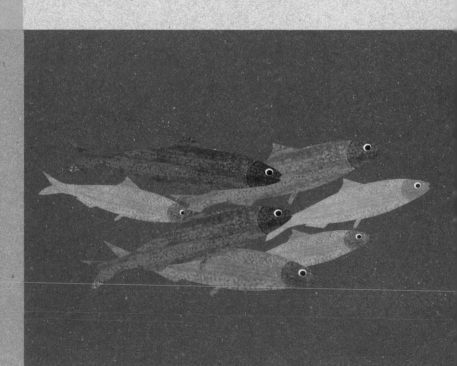

FISH
EVERYWHERE

BRITTA TECKENTRUP

B P P

THERE ARE FISH EVERYWHERE

Fish live all over the world. They can be found in oceans, rivers, lakes, ponds, or anywhere with enough water. They can be big or small, spiny or flat, spiky or blobby, bright or exactly the same color as the sand, making them really hard to see. These are all fish . . . aren't they?*

Sailfish

Trumpetfish

Anchovy

Angelfish

Shark

Dolphin

Moray eel

Squirrelfish

Crab

Blenny

Sea star

Sea turtle

Dolphinfish

Eagle ray

Eagle ray

Royal dottyback

Seahorse

Sea turtle

Arapaima

Piranha

Ocean sunfish

Lionfish

Plaice

Salmon

*You're right! Some of these are NOT fish and we put them here to make sure you're awake. Can you guess which ones are NOT fish?

IT'S A FISH!
(SO WHAT *IS* THAT?)

Fish are a type of animal that lives in water. They are vertebrates, which means they have backbones. All fish have a brain, and most use gills to breathe and fins to steer. They are also usually cold-blooded (meaning their body temperature varies with their environment), and many are covered in scales.

BONY FISH

At least 29,000 species of fish are **bony fish**—that's half of all vertebrate species on the planet. These fish have a bony skeleton.

Dorsal fin

Kidney

Liver

Brain

Nostril

Swim bladder

Bony skeleton

Barbel

Caudal fin

Gills

Heart

Stomach

Anal fin

Reproductive organs

Pelvic fin

Intestine

Pectoral fin

UP AND DOWN!
(OR HOW THE SWIM BLADDER WORKS)

Many bony fish have a swim bladder—a sac filled with gas, which the fish can use to go up and down in the water.

When a fish relaxes the muscles around the swim bladder, the bladder expands and the fish rises.

When a fish tightens muscles around the swim bladder, the bladder gets smaller and the fish sinks.

IT'S NOT A FISH

Did you guess which of the creatures on the previous pages weren't fish?

Turtles are **reptiles.** Reptiles are cold-blooded vertebrates with dry, scaly skin. They lay their eggs on land.

Sea stars are **echinoderms.** Echinoderms are invertebrates (creatures without a backbone) with a hard external covering.

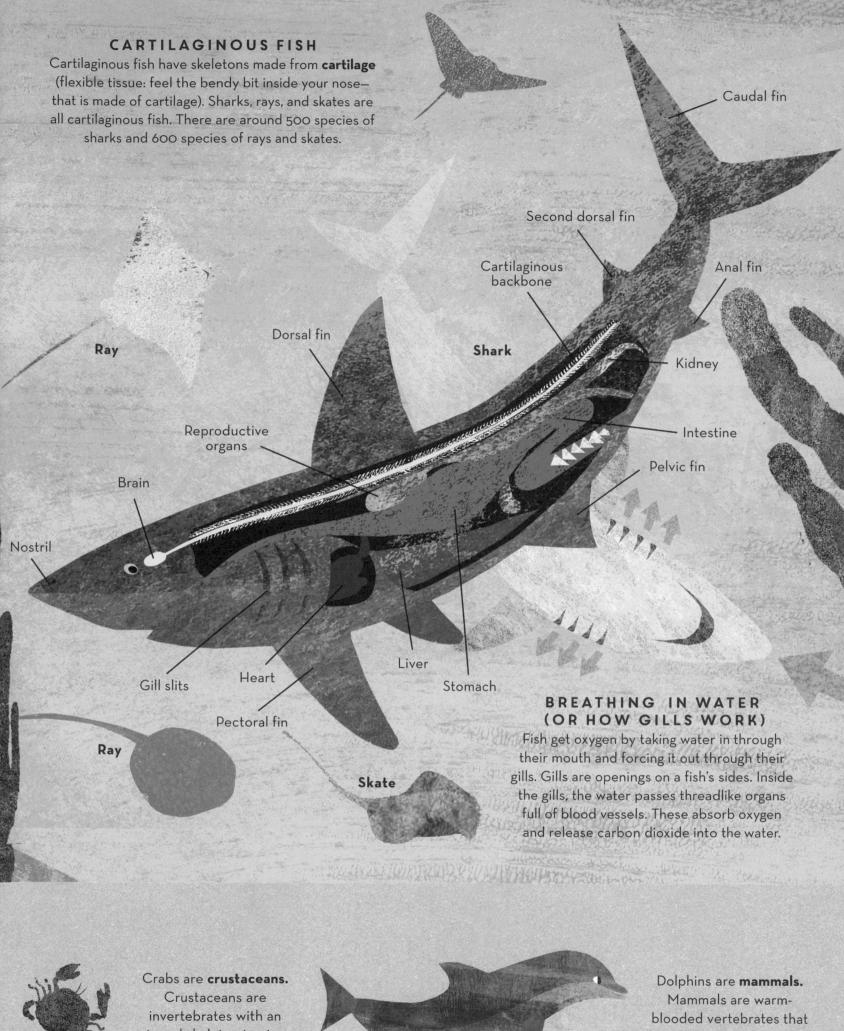

CARTILAGINOUS FISH

Cartilaginous fish have skeletons made from **cartilage** (flexible tissue: feel the bendy bit inside your nose—that is made of cartilage). Sharks, rays, and skates are all cartilaginous fish. There are around 500 species of sharks and 600 species of rays and skates.

Caudal fin

Second dorsal fin

Cartilaginous backbone

Anal fin

Dorsal fin

Ray

Shark

Kidney

Reproductive organs

Intestine

Brain

Pelvic fin

Nostril

Liver

Stomach

Gill slits

Heart

Ray

Pectoral fin

Skate

BREATHING IN WATER (OR HOW GILLS WORK)

Fish get oxygen by taking water in through their mouth and forcing it out through their gills. Gills are openings on a fish's sides. Inside the gills, the water passes threadlike organs full of blood vessels. These absorb oxygen and release carbon dioxide into the water.

Crabs are **crustaceans.** Crustaceans are invertebrates with an external skeleton in pieces (like armor) and antennae.

Dolphins are **mammals.** Mammals are warm-blooded vertebrates that feed their young with milk. (YOU are a mammal!)

FISH HAVE BEEN AROUND FOR AGES

Fish have been everywhere for a really long time. Scientists believe that there were fish on Earth for around 100 million years before animals with legs. The Devonian period (410 to 360 million years ago) is often called the Age of Fish because it's when some of the most important fish evolution occurred.

The first fish we know about are the jawless fish, which appeared around 500 million years ago. Some, like **Hemicyclaspis,** had an armor-like outer skeleton.

Hagfish are living fossils in today's oceans. Their ancestors may have lived 500 million years ago. Hagfish produce a sticky slime to ward off predators.

500 million years ago

Hemicyclaspis

Hagfish

Lamprey

Lampreys are the only surviving jawless fish. They use their toothy mouth to attach themselves to a prey animal and suck its blood.

Spiny sharks were some of the earliest jawed fish. They lived 438 to 258 million years ago and are not true sharks—they have features of both sharks and bony fish.

The first true shark we know much about is **Leonodus,** which lived around 400 million years ago. All scientists have found to prove it existed are fossils of its teeth.

Spiny shark

Leonodus **teeth**

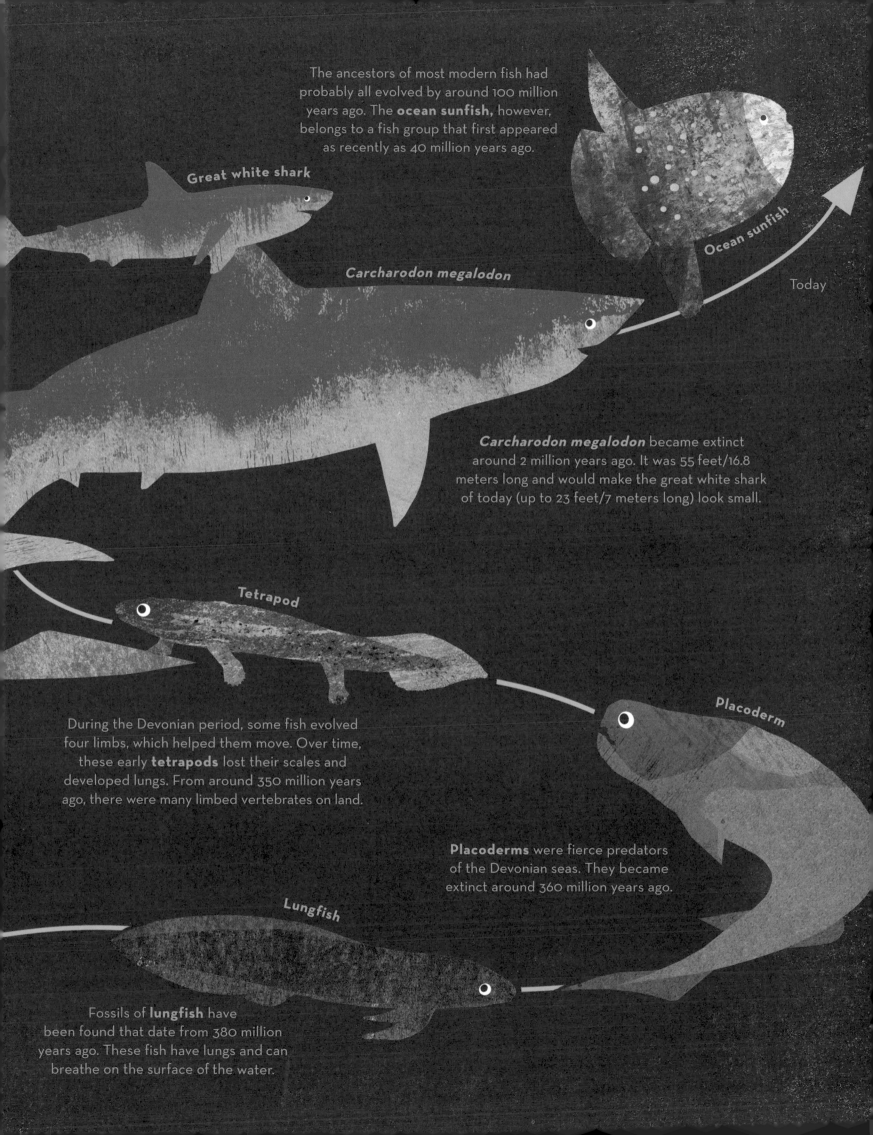

The ancestors of most modern fish had probably all evolved by around 100 million years ago. The **ocean sunfish,** however, belongs to a fish group that first appeared as recently as 40 million years ago.

Great white shark

Carcharodon megalodon

Ocean sunfish

Today

Carcharodon megalodon became extinct around 2 million years ago. It was 55 feet/16.8 meters long and would make the great white shark of today (up to 23 feet/7 meters long) look small.

Tetrapod

Placoderm

During the Devonian period, some fish evolved four limbs, which helped them move. Over time, these early **tetrapods** lost their scales and developed lungs. From around 350 million years ago, there were many limbed vertebrates on land.

Placoderms were fierce predators of the Devonian seas. They became extinct around 360 million years ago.

Lungfish

Fossils of **lungfish** have been found that date from 380 million years ago. These fish have lungs and can breathe on the surface of the water.

FRESHWATER FISH

Nearly 40 percent of the world's fish species live in fresh water (water that isn't salty like the ocean). This is despite the fact that only 1 percent of the world's water is fresh. Freshwater fish live in lakes, rivers, ponds, swamps, and even hot springs and caves.

Antarctica and Australia, the driest continents on Earth, have the fewest freshwater fish. Australia has more than 300 native species. Antarctica has none at all (although fossils of freshwater fish have been found there that are hundreds of millions of years old).

The **tambaqui** eats leaves and fruit from plants near the water. Its poop spreads seeds around the Amazon rain forest.

Tambaqui

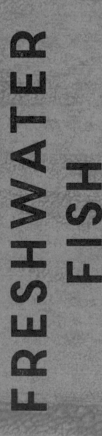

The MONSTER-size **arapaima** can grow more than 10 feet/3 meters long.

Arapaima

THE AMAZON RIVER

The Amazon River begins in the Andes Mountains of South America and flows 2,500 miles/4,000 kilometers to the Atlantic Ocean. At the river's mouth, salt and fresh water mingle for more than 100 miles/160 kilometers. The Amazon and the streams that feed it contain more than 3,000 species of fish. Many migrate long distances, including the dorado catfish, which can travel 7,200 miles/11,600 kilometers. That's like swimming between London and New York and back again!

Red-bellied piranha

UNEXPECTED PLACES

Some freshwater fish live in places you'd never imagine were possible.

Red-bellied piranhas can strip their prey of flesh in minutes. Their teeth are so sharp that some indigenous Amazon people use them as weapons.

In caves: Mexican blind cavefish have lived underground so long that they have evolved without eyes! Being sightless helps them conserve energy.

In the desert: The Devils Hole pupfish is found in only one underground pool in Death Valley, Nevada—the hottest place on Earth.

On land (some of the time): Mudskippers live in swamps and walk with their fins. They breathe through their special skin.

Under ice: Burbots live in regions near the North Pole. They are one of the few fish that lay their eggs under ice.

Bull sharks are one of the few sharks that can live in salt and fresh water. They swim from the ocean far up rivers.

Bull shark

Dorado catfish

Dorado catfish live on the murky Amazon riverbed and use their barbels (the parts that look like a cat's whiskers) to feel their way and find food.

THE DEEP BLUE SEA

The Earth is covered in water. Salty oceans cover around 70 percent of the planet's surface and contain 97 percent of its water. Different parts of the ocean are home to different types of fish—from tiny creatures darting in tide pools to ghostly deep-sea dwellers.

THE OPEN OCEAN

FISH THAT LIVE IN THE OPEN OCEAN ARE OFTEN LARGE, MUSCULAR, AND FAST. UP TO AROUND 660 FEET/200 METERS BELOW THE SURFACE, ENOUGH LIGHT COMES THROUGH THE WATER TO ALLOW FOR PHOTOSYNTHESIS (THE PROCESS BY WHICH PLANTS MAKE FOOD USING SUNLIGHT).

Anchovies swim with their mouth open to catch plankton.

Anchovies

Sleek, fast-moving fish like **tuna** hunt smaller fish like anchovies.

The **ocean sunfish** weighs up to 5,100 pounds/2,300 kilograms and is the heaviest bony fish.

Ocean sunfish

Tuna

Zooplankton

Phytoplankton live in the top 660 feet/200 meters of the ocean. Many fish eat them, and so do very small marine animals called **zooplankton**.

Sailfish

Sailfish (which can be 11 feet/3.3 meters long) are the world's fastest fish. They can swim at an incredible 68 miles/110 kilometers per hour.

THE TWILIGHT ZONE

THE TWILIGHT ZONE LIES BETWEEN 660 FEET/200 METERS AND 3,300 FEET/1,000 METERS BELOW THE SURFACE OF THE WATER.

MARINE SHALLOWS

MANY TYPES OF FISH LIVE NEAR THE SHORE. SHALLOW AREAS PROVIDE SAFE PLACES FOR FISH TO LAY THEIR EGGS OR HIDE IN ROCKS.

The **black swallower** can swallow fish a whopping ten times its own size.

In 2014, scientists saw a ghostly **snailfish** at 26,000 feet/8,000 meters deep in the Mariana Trench. Humans are only just beginning to understand the variety of life in the oceans.

Snailfish

Black swallower

Spotted lantern fish

Many deep-sea creatures, like the **spotted lantern fish**, the **gulper eel**, and the **anglerfish**, make their own light by a chemical reaction called bioluminescence.

Gulper eel

Tripod fish

Anglerfish

The **tripod fish** has long "stilts," which put it at the perfect height for food like krill to swim into its mouth.

At greater depths, **water** is under higher pressure. Deep-sea fish have pressure-resistant bodies, but if they come too close to the surface, their swim bladder can expand and kill them.

DEEPER STILL

AT 3,300 FT/1,000 METERS AND DEEPER, IT IS COMPLETELY DARK. FISH THAT LIVE HERE HAVE EVOLVED SPECIAL ADAPTATIONS THAT ENABLE THEM TO SURVIVE WHERE LIGHT AND FOOD ARE SCARCE.

CAN YOU FIND IT?

Atlantic cod lay their eggs in coastal areas but can also be found as deep as 2,000 feet/600 meters beneath the surface. **Can you find all the Atlantic cod in this picture?**

THE CORAL REEF

Beneath the ocean's warm, tropical waters, you will find colorful coral reefs. Coral reefs cover less than one percent of Earth's surface, but around a quarter of all sea creatures live there. Put on your diving goggles and peer beneath the water—what will you see?

Yellow longnose butterfly fish

Coral might look like plants, but they are animals. What looks to us like a small tree is made up of thousands of tiny creatures called polyps.

There are around 130 species of **butterfly fish.**

Black-backed butterfly fish

Some coral use their "arms" to catch food. Others have microscopic plants called **algae** living inside them. The algae make food for themselves and the coral.

Double-saddle butterfly fish

Layers of dead coral form **rocky reefs** on which new coral grows.

Mandarin fish smell horrible! They have poisonous spines and a smelly mucus coating to protect them from predators.

Mandarin fish

Just like a parrot, the **Pacific longnose parrotfish** has a beak. It uses it to grind coral where the algae it eats are found.

Male parrotfish

Female parrotfish

CAN YOU FIND IT?
Male, female, and juvenile parrotfish look different from one another. **Can you find one more of each on this page?**

Juvenile parrotfish

Orange-spotted filefish

Blue surgeonfish

Moorish idol

Clown fish

Clown fish live near sea anemones to avoid predators. The fish's mucus layer protects them from the anemone's sting.

Watch out for the **blacktip reef shark** if you're a fish! Reefs are full of food for predators like sharks and moray eels.

Hedgehog seahorse

Moray eel

FEEDING

In the world of fish, the greatest daily challenge is finding enough to eat. And fish eat a huge variety of food—everything from microscopic algae and marine creatures to . . . each other. Much of how fish behave and where they live is based on where they can find the food they need to survive.

FROM SMALL TO BIG — THE OCEAN FOOD CHAIN

3. The ocean is also home to many plant-eating fish (**herbivores**), which eat algae and seagrasses. Damselfish even tend algae farms! And many fish are **omnivores,** eating both plants and animals.

2. Phytoplankton are eaten by **zooplankton,** tiny marine animals, and by other animals, such as jellyfish.

1. Tiny plants called **phytoplankton** are among the smallest living things in the ocean. They often live near the surface, where they soak up the sun's energy.

4. Fish that only eat other animals are known as **carnivores.** Some, like sardines and herrings, eat zooplankton. Other carnivorous fish eat smaller fish, crabs, or shellfish.

5. The biggest **predators** in the ocean include fish such as large sharks and tuna, mammals such as dolphins and seals, and birds such as penguins.

WEIRD AND WONDERFUL FEEDERS

Meet some of the fish world's most innovative eaters.

Like humans, fish have taste buds on their tongue, but some fish also have them on their face or body. **Catfish** have up to 175,000 taste buds (compared to humans' mere 10,000), most of which are on their barbels—the fleshy feelers that look like a cat's whiskers.

Catfish

Archerfish

Archerfish know how to spit! They spit a powerful jet of water at insects to bring them down into the water.

Sharks have cells on their head that can detect electric fields. This sense is called electroreception.

Shark

The largest fish in the ocean eats some of the smallest food! **Whale sharks** (which can be 40 feet/12 meters long) prefer to eat tiny plankton, which they filter out of the water they suck into their huge mouths.

Whale shark

Much like human fishermen, **anglerfish** dangle a lure in the water to attract prey. The lure is a special light organ on the fish's head.

Anglerfish

Electric eel

Electric eels stun their prey with an electric shock of up to 600 volts.

STAYING ALIVE

Underwater, it's a fish-eat-fish world. Smaller, weaker fish are constantly threatened by hungry predators. Many have evolved amazing ways to avoid being eaten—from simply becoming very good at hiding to forming surprising relationships with other creatures.

CAN YOU FIND IT?

Some fish have adapted to look exactly like their environments. Can you find these masters of disguise?

Leaf scorpion fish

Large-tooth flounder

Yellow-crested weed fish

Leafy sea dragon

Stonefish*

*Be careful! This is one of the most poisonous fish on Earth!

MASTERS OF SURVIVAL

Fish don't just rely on camouflage. There are many other ways they have learned to survive.

MAKING EYES

Some small fish, such as some kinds of **damselfish,** have an eye-shaped marking on their fin. This confuses larger fish about which end of the damselfish to attack and which way it is swimming.

CHEMICAL WEAPONS

When it is threatened, the **white-spotted boxfish** releases a poison that is strong enough to kill other fish.

I'M BIGGER THAN YOU THOUGHT!

Spotted porcupine fish have a special escape tactic. If they are threatened by a predator, they can fill their stomach with water, puff up to more than twice their regular size, and extend their fierce spines.

Before

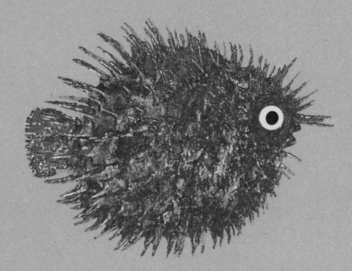

After

TRAVELING COMPANIONS

Some fish develop special relationships with toxic sea anemones or jellyfish to keep predators at bay. Juvenile **golden trevally** can often be found in jellyfish tentacles.

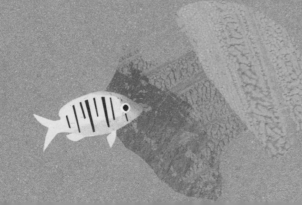

HIDE-AND-SEEK

Many fish hide in rocks, plants, or reefs. **Squirrelfish** hide during the day and come out at night. They make clicking, grunting noises to scare off predators.

SCHOOLING

Another way fish avoid predators is by swimming in schools. What is a school of fish? (And, no, it's not where fish learn math.) A school is a group of fish that all swim together in the same direction and in a tight formation.

Fish swim in schools to **confuse predators**. A moving mass of fish looks like a bigger creature and makes it hard for a predator to single out its prey.

Fish swimming at the back need **less energy** to swim because they are helped by water movement made by the fish at the front.

Indian mimic goatfish

CAN YOU FIND IT?
Indian mimic goatfish look a bit like bluestripe snappers and often school with them to hide from predators.

Can you find all the goatfish in this school?

Bluestripe snapper

Bluestripe snappers are found in tropical waters. They school near reefs, caves, and shipwrecks. Fish usually school with fish from the same species. They recognize one another by their scent.

Hungry fish may swim at the front or on the outer edges of the school, even though it is more dangerous, because it's easier to find food from these positions.

Scientists have discovered that fish with **speedy reaction times** are more likely to lead a school.

Schools of fish can **change direction quickly** to avoid predators.

FISH PARENTS

Fish mate, lay their eggs, and care for their young in all sorts of different ways. Many fish lay eggs that are fertilized outside their bodies, while some give birth to live young. Some fish let their eggs drift in the tide, while others build elaborate nests, which they defend aggressively. Fish parents have adapted to give the next generation the best chance of survival.

RAISING THE ODDS

Many fish that live in the open ocean lay their eggs by spawning—the female fish release their eggs into the water, where they are fertilized by males. Every year, billions of **sardines** gather in a huge school near South Africa to spawn. Sardine eggs drift in the ocean, and parents do not care for their young.

ELABORATE COURTSHIP

Some fish have elaborate courtship rituals. This **Japanese puffer fish** is thought to create an intricate pattern in the sand to attract a mate.

HE TO SHE

Some fish even change sex as part of their reproductive process. **Clown fish** are all born male and live in groups with one dominant female. When she dies, a male will change to a female to take her place.

MOUTH NURSERY

Some female **African cichlids** keep their eggs in their mouth for up to 36 days. Young fish will still seek protection in their mother's mouth.

DANCING PARTNERS

Male and female **seahorses** perform a courtship dance before they mate. This can be a feat of endurance, as it may last up to eight hours!

SEAHORSE DADS

Male **seahorses** have a pouch in their belly where they receive the female's eggs during mating. Baby seahorses stay there until they are ready to come out.

LIVE YOUNG

Not all fish lay eggs. Many **sharks** and **rays** and some other types of fish give birth to live young.

MERMAIDS' PURSES

Some **sharks, rays,** and **skates** do lay eggs. Their egg cases sometimes wash up on beaches— beachcombers call them mermaids' purses.

PROTECTIVE PARENTING

Male **Garibaldi fish** build nests in coral reefs. A female lays her eggs in a nest— and is then quickly chased away by the male! He will continue to guard the nest fiercely.

ATLANTIC SALMON

Atlantic salmon go to great lengths to breed—literally! They may migrate many thousands of miles. Adult salmon live in the freezing waters of the North Atlantic Ocean near Greenland. After one to four years at sea, they return to the rivers where they were born in Europe, North America, and Russia. Here they lay their eggs. Young salmon return to the sea, and the cycle begins all over again.

Male salmon turn orange, and their heads change shape.

Breeding female

Breeding male

Female salmon become dark green with blue and purple on their sides.

Salmon enter rivers between **April and November.** At this point, they begin to look very different and stop eating.

Adult salmon are silvery gray. At sea, they feed on small fish.

Adult salmon

CAN YOU FIND
all the predators looking for salmon to eat?

Despite not having a map, salmon manage to swim back to the rivers where they were born. Scientists believe they navigate by **magnetic fields** while at sea and by **smell** and **taste** in rivers.

When salmon reach the area they were born in, between **October and January,** they lay their eggs. Female salmon bury their eggs in riverbed gravel.

The **eggs** are fertilized by males as they are released.

Newly hatched salmon are called **alevins.**

Once the alevins have absorbed the yolk sacs that protrude from their bodies, they are known as **fry.**

By the end of summer, the fish are around 1.5 inches/4 centimeters long with dark markings. They are now called **parr.**

After two or three years, the parr turn silvery and are called **smolts.** In spring, smolts swim downriver to the sea.

Alevin

Fry

Parr

Eggs

Smolt

FISH AND PEOPLE

Fish have been an important source of food for humans for thousands of years. Many people are also fascinated by the behavior of fish or prize them for their beautiful colors. And now scientists are seeking new species deep beneath the ocean's surface.

ICE FISHING
Some cultures have developed ways of **fishing** in even the most hostile environments. The Inuit people of Alaska and Canada catch fish through holes in the ice during winter.

FISHING TACKLE
Early humans developed technology to catch fish. The earliest known **fishhooks** were found on the island of Okinawa, in Japan; they are thought to be 23,000 years old.

PRETTY PETS
Have you ever had a **goldfish**? Keeping goldfish as pets was common among wealthy people in ninth-century China.

ANCIENT RECIPE
The city of Pompeii was famous for making **garum,** a fish sauce that was very popular in ancient Rome. To make garum, mash fish together with their eggs and entrails. Then leave the mixture for six weeks until it has fermented. Yum!

PROTECTED PLACES

A **marine reserve** is a part of the ocean where fishing is not allowed and the natural environment is protected. The largest marine reserve is in Antarctica's Ross Sea. Fish, penguins, whales, and other creatures go there to feed on krill.

TAKING TOO MUCH?

The world's biggest fishing trawler can catch 400 million tons/360 million metric tons of fish in 24 hours. The populations of some ocean species have been greatly reduced by such large-scale commercial fishing: these species are caught in the trawlers' nets, but as they can't be sold, they're discarded.

PLASTIC SOUP

Do you really need a straw with your drink? Plastic items like this end up in our oceans and are **endangering marine life.** More than 12 million tons/11 million metric tons of plastic may be added to the ocean every year. You can help by reducing the amount of plastic you use and by recycling.

NEW LIFE?

New species of marine animals are discovered every year. Scientists exploring the Mariana Trench, the deepest place in the ocean, use special robots like *Nereus* to observe life in the deep.

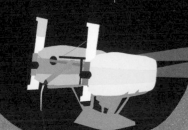